i

AMERICAN STEAMBOAT TOWN
A Paper Model Kit

Based on the Buildings of
Historical La Center, Washington
Showing the Riverside buildings
and the LaCenter Steamboat.

Created by
Don Landes-McCullough

Thanks to the La Center Museum and Barbara Barnhart
for access to the historical photos used in this project.

Special thanks go to Jack Fillman,
the man who preserved so much of the
history of the town of La Center, WA.

The La Center Museum is not in any way responsble for this project,
which remains the sole responsibility of Don Landes-McCullough
and HeyUKid!

Publishing Company: Parasol Publishing
Children's Division: HeyUKid!
A Division of Don James Art
Printed by: Create Space

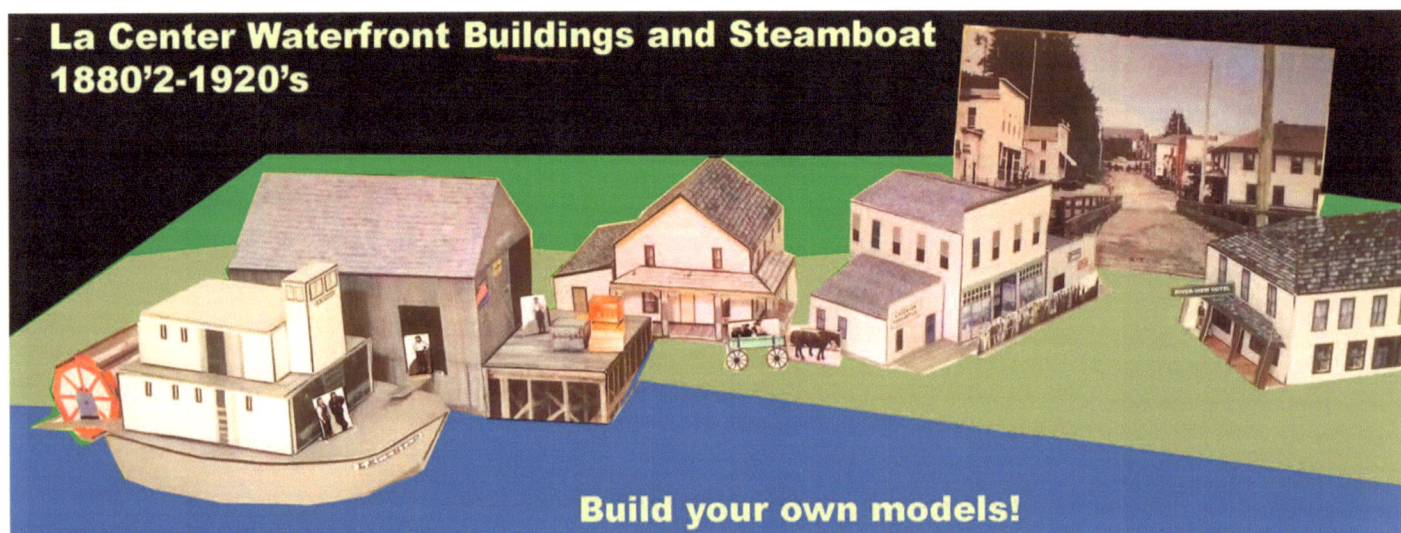

La Center Waterfront Buildings and Steamboat 1880'2-1920's

Build your own models!

Welcome to a real Steamboat Town on the North Fork of the Lewis River around the time of 1880's to the 1920's. La Center, Washington

Dock Building

House by Dock

Hobert Store

River-View Hotel

La Center, Washington Waterfront Late 1800's to Early 1900's

This is a photograph of the town at one time during that period. The buildings that are labeled are the ones that you can construct from this fun kit. You will also be able to create a simplified copy of the Steamboat "La Center." If you want to get really creative, you can add your own details or make it into a diorama (it was all set on a hill going up from the river.)

Have fun!

Created by
Don Landes-McCullough
for

heyUkid

Instructions and hints

TOOLS: Scissors, glue, tape, scoring tool (see #2 below.)

1) Cut out each piece.

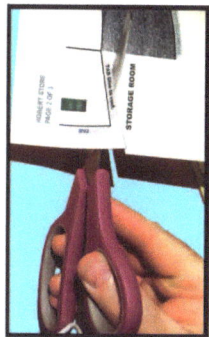

-You may remove the book staples or just cut out each picture.
-It is best to only cut out the pieces for one building at a time.

Build your own models!

2) Score all the black lines.

All solid black lines show you where to fold the paper. "Scoring" means to take a pointed object that is not too sharp (you don't want to cut your lines, just indent them) and make a pressed outline along every black line. This makes it easy to fold the black lines exactly where you have scored (creased) them. This is especially important when working with small details. Do this to all black lines before you begin folding the pieces, and your work will be much easier. Try using a butter knife, a fork sprong, etc.

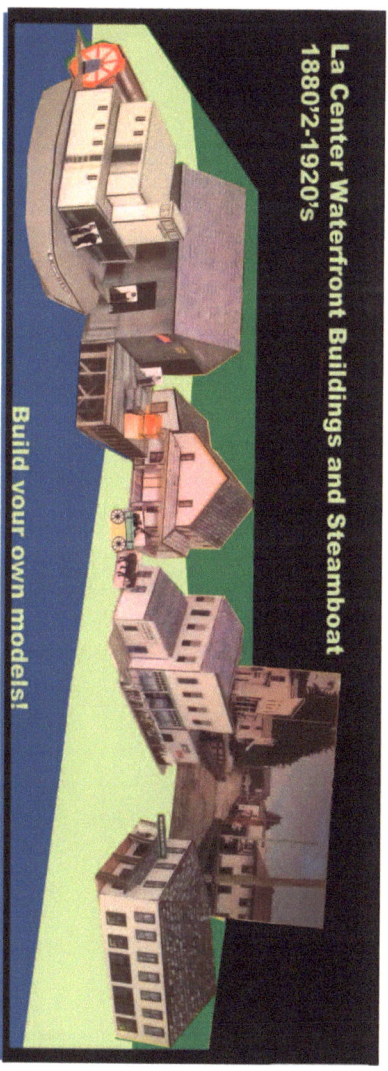

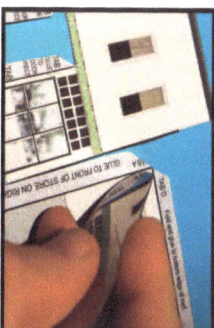

Using a butter knife.

~SCORING~

Using a fork tip.

3) Begin by gluing the main wall sections together.

Most of the objects are made like boxes, including most of the Steamboat. Lay out the wall sections and make sure you have four sides and a roof. Because some of the buildings are bigger than the paper length, you have to put the four walls together yourself. Some walls are in two sections that glue together to make four walls. Some walls need to add a fourth section to the end of three sections. Glue the walls into one strip and then fold them to make the box.

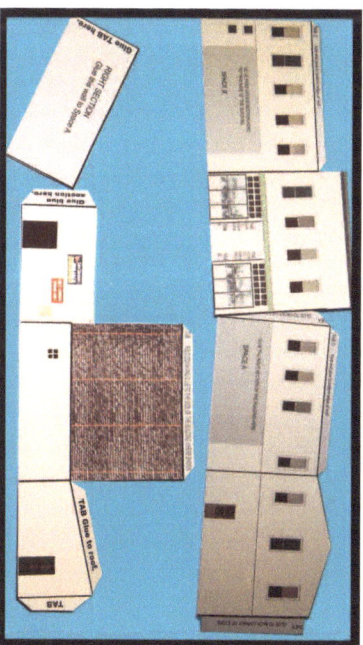

Most buildings require that you make four walls by gluing two sections together.

4) Glue the TABs into their places.

As you fold the pieces, they will begin to show you where the TABs should go. Most tabs have angled ends because it makes the ends go under the folded pieces more easily.

5) To make the people and animals:

Fold the two photos back to back. Glue them together. Fold out the colored TABs on the bottom to create a stand.

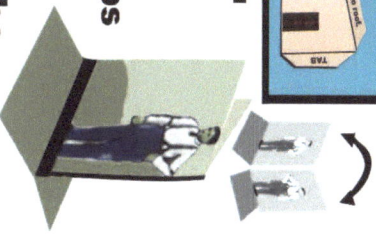

3

TOWN PHOTO FOR DIORAMA

Cut out the photo. Glue the Standup pieces to the back of this photo to make it stand. It will make a great backdrop for your La Center models.

5

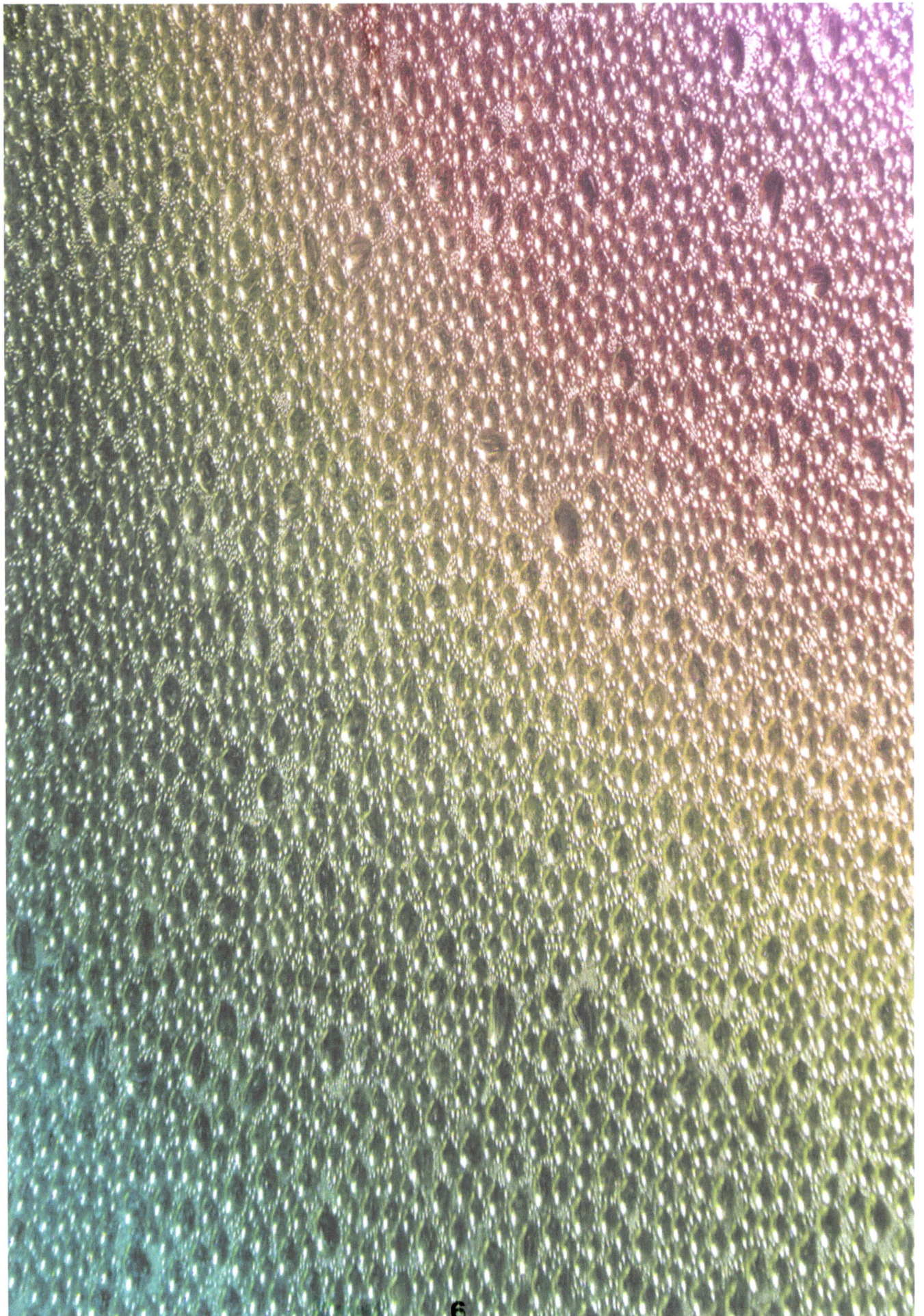

RIVER-VIEW HOTEL

Glue the door as shown here.

DOOR
Cut out Door and glue to the blue TABs. It will be angled across corner.

This photo is the finished model of the River-view Hotel.

Photo of the real River-View Hotel

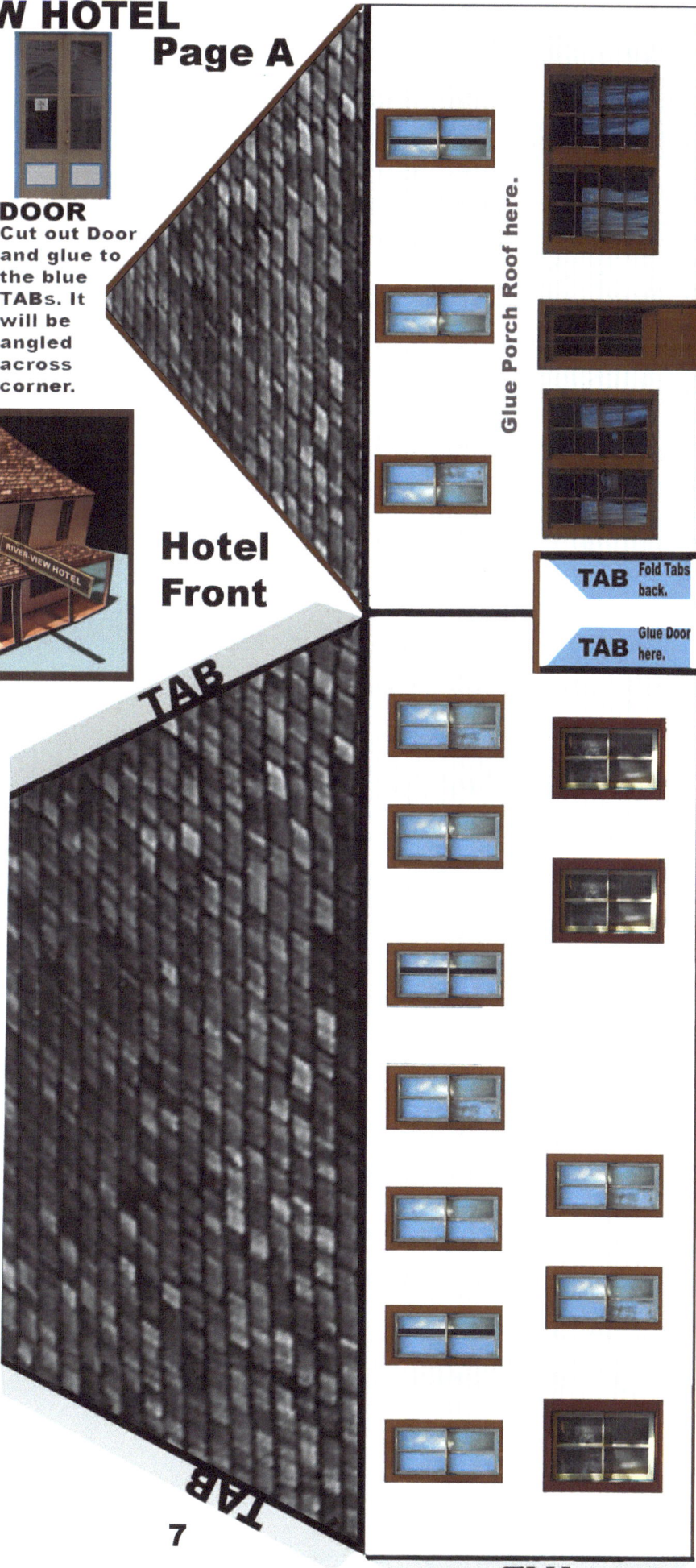

Glue Porch Roof here.

This is the Hotel Boardwalk, Fold it out and glue it to the TAB floor of the Porch.

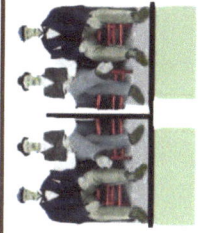

Hotel Front

TAB

TAB — Fold Tabs back.

TAB — Glue Door here.

Hotel Guests sitting on the front porch.

RIVER-VIEW HOTEL

RIVER-VIEW HOTEL

SIGN - Fold in half, then glue to front of Hotel above the porch.

Fold TABs to glue to wall.

TAB

TAB

7

8

RIVER-VIEW HOTEL Page B

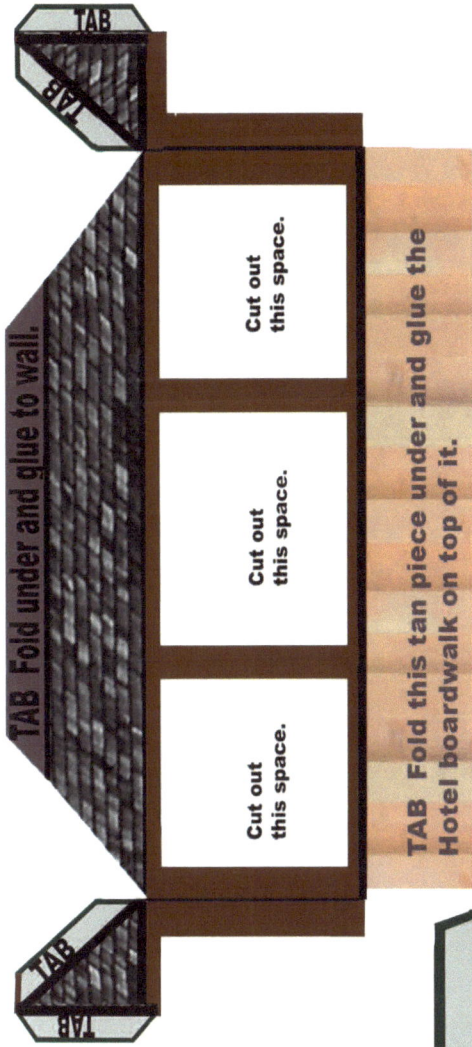

BACK END

TAB Fold under and glue to wall.

Cut out this space.

Cut out this space.

Cut out this space.

TAB Fold this tan piece under and glue the Hotel boardwalk on top of it.

TAB

TAB

TAB

TAB

TAB

TAB

TAB

Hobert Store

River-View Hotel

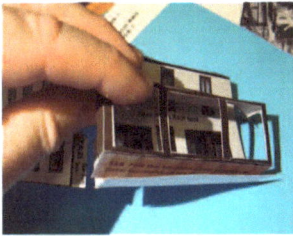

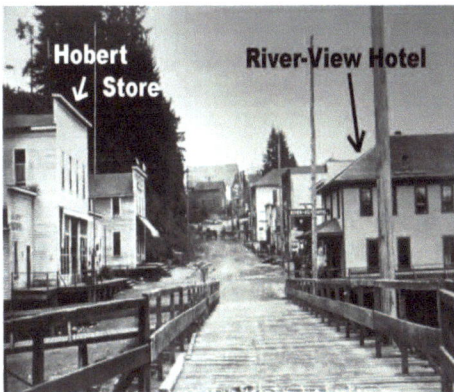

Photo of the real River-View Hotel

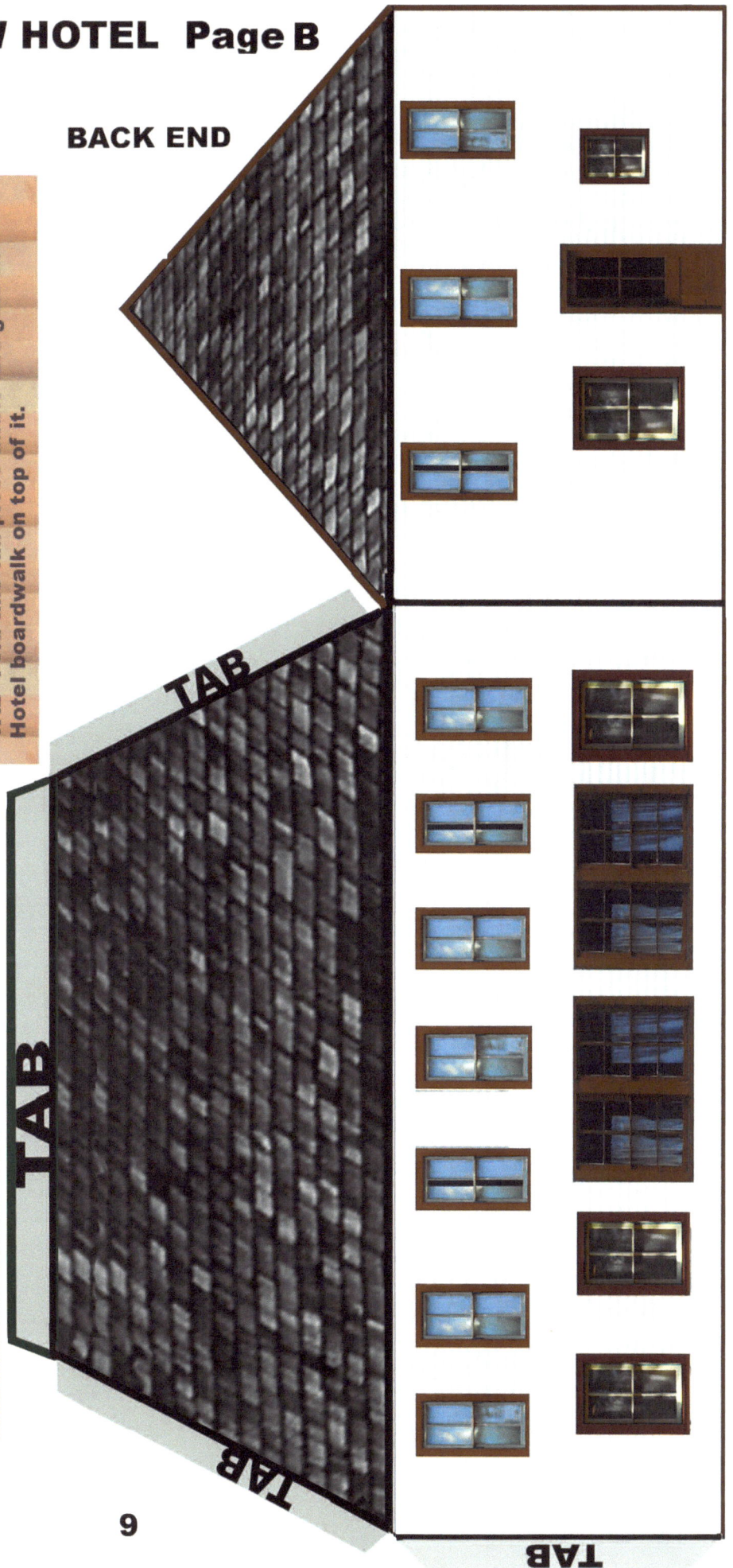

Front Side Piece (toward the river.)

Tab

Cut out slot.

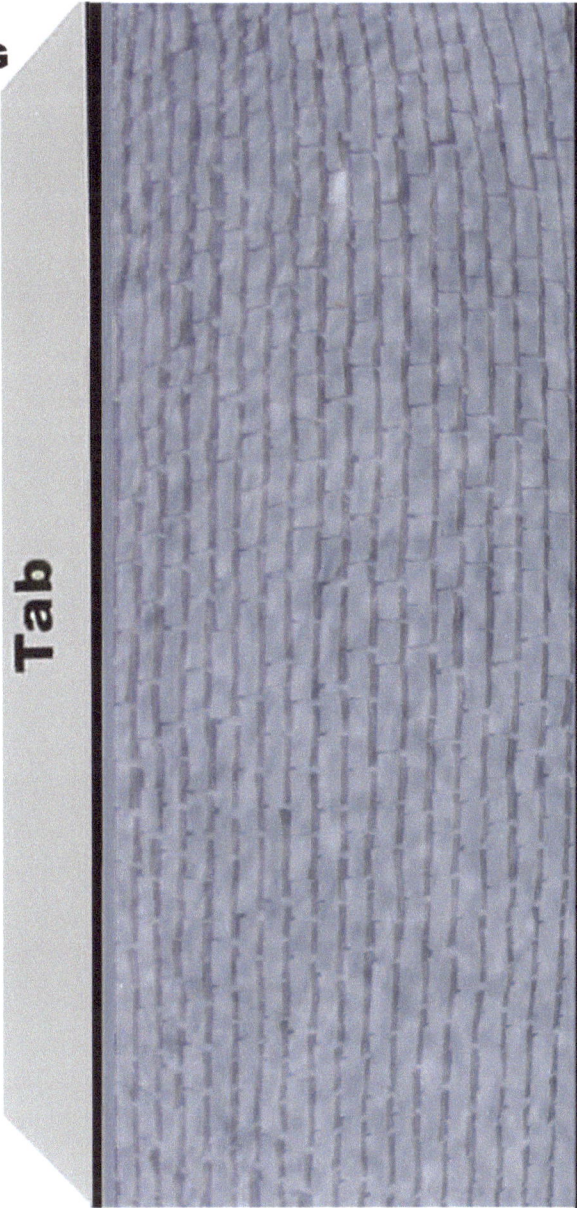

Man standing at the
top of the Gangplank.

This is a
photo of the
finished
model of the
Dock Building.

Tab

Tab

11

Tab   Glue to back.

DOCK
BUILDING
Page B

Back Side Piece (away from the river.)

Photos of
the real dock
with the Steamboat
"La Center" in
1912 and in
1917 after it
was remodelled.

1917

1912

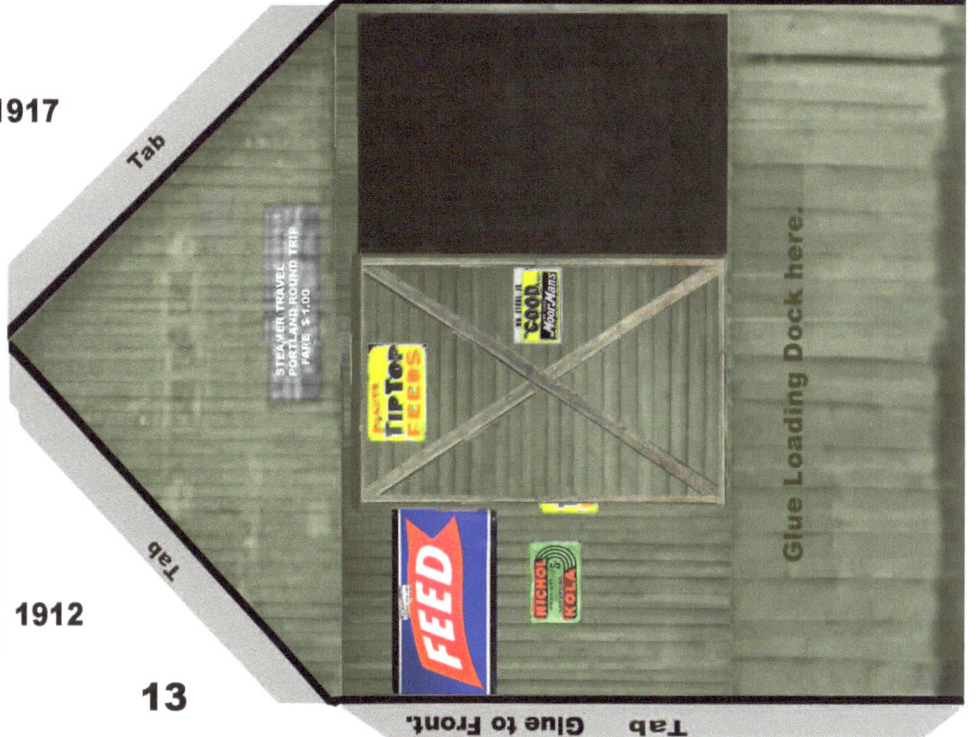

Tab

Tab

Tab

Glue to Front.

Glue Loading Dock here.

STEAMER TRAVEL
PORTLAND ROUND TRIP
FARE $ 1.00

TIP TOP FEEDS

FEED

NICHOL KOLA

13

DOCK
BUILDING
Page C

LOADING DOCK

Glue this side to wall.

TAB

Tab

Tab

Tab

Tab

TAB

**Fold and
glue into
a box shape.**

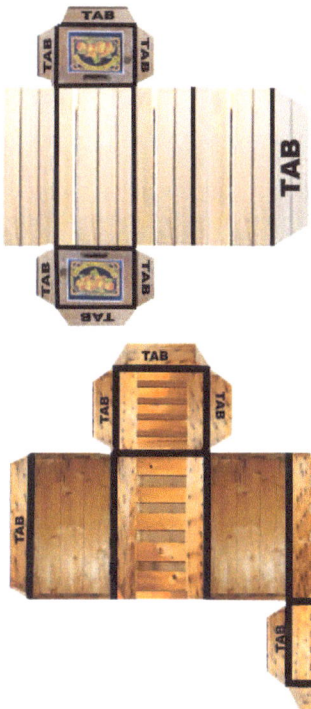

These are boxes
and trunks waiting
to be shipped by
steamboat. Fold
and glue each
one into a
box shape.

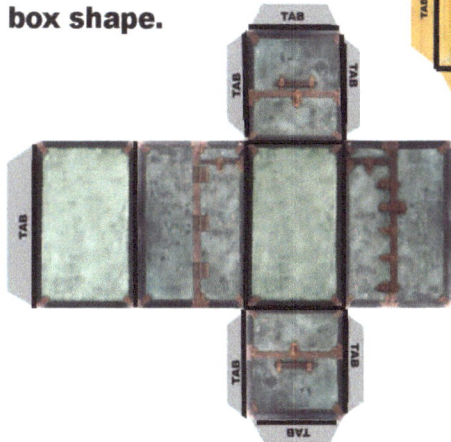

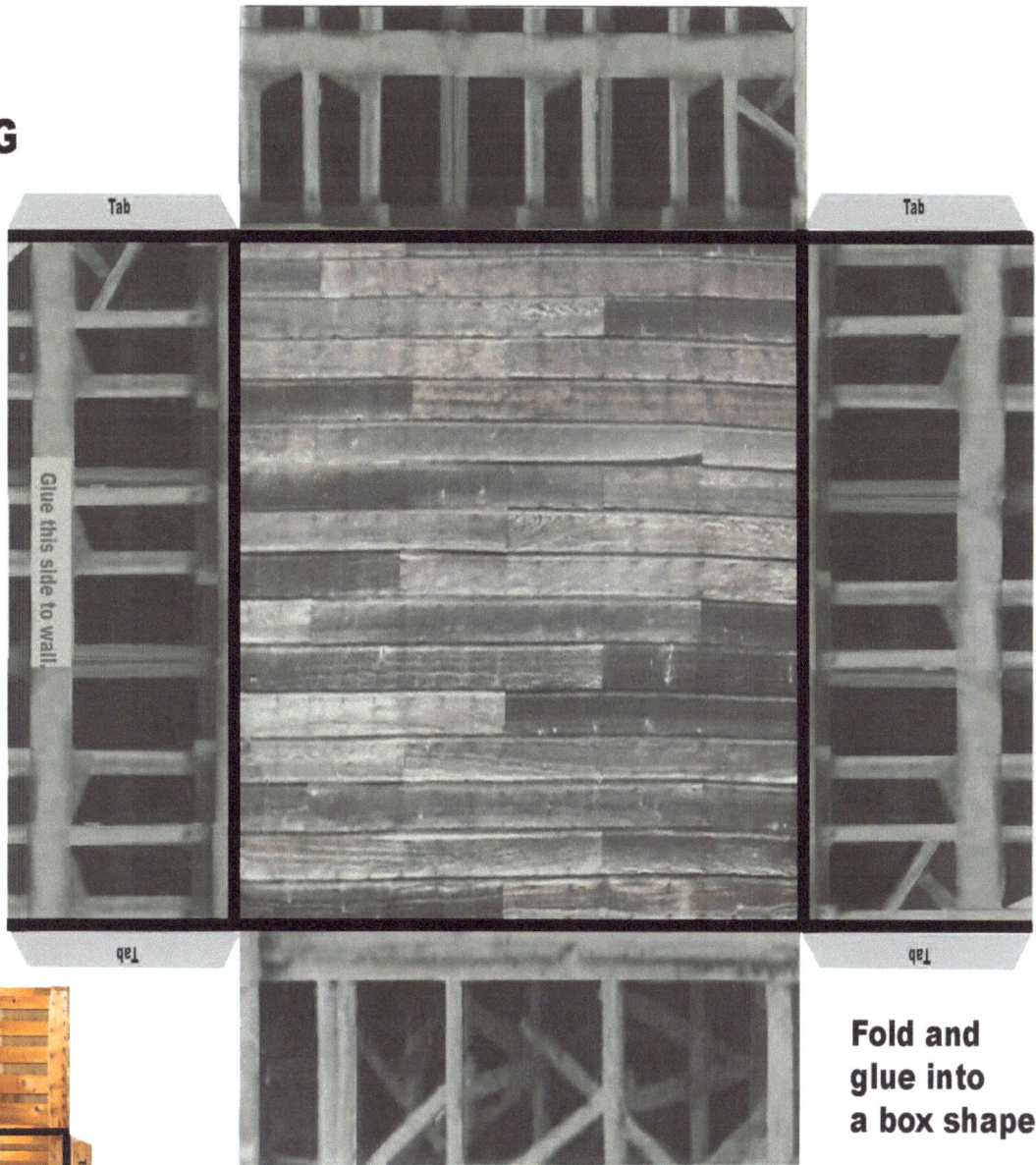

TAB

Gang
Plank

TAB

**Put this
end into
the slot
in the front
of the
building.
The other
end goes
onto the
deck of
the boat.**

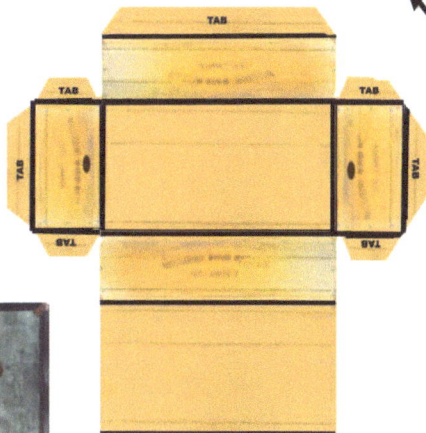

15

Dock Worker

DOCK HOUSE
Page A

Fold Porch Floor and glue on top of Porch Roof TAB.

Poor Floor

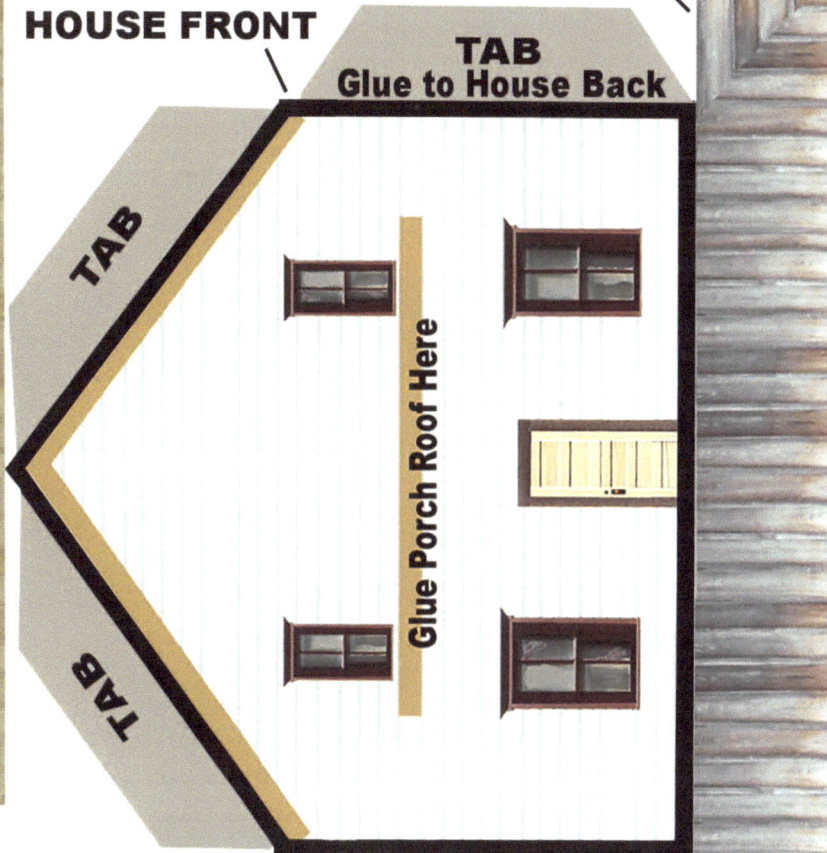

HOUSE FRONT

TAB

TAB Glue to House Back

TAB

TAB

Glue Porch Roof Here

PORCH RAIL PIECE 1
Glue this end TAB to the Porch Rail Piece 2.

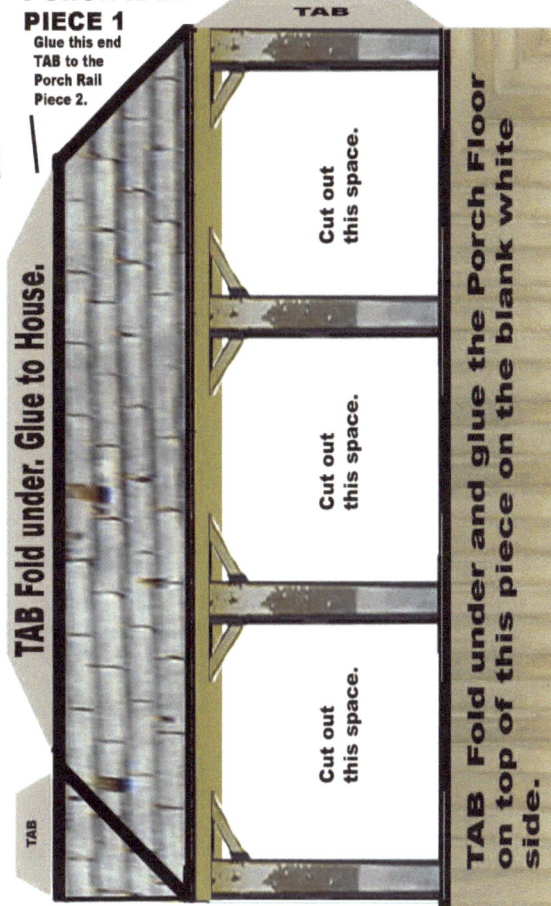

TAB

Cut out this space.

Cut out this space.

Cut out this space.

TAB Fold under. Glue to House.

TAB Fold under and glue the Porch Floor on top of this piece on the blank white side.

TAB

TAB

DOCK HOUSE
Photo of the real Dock House.

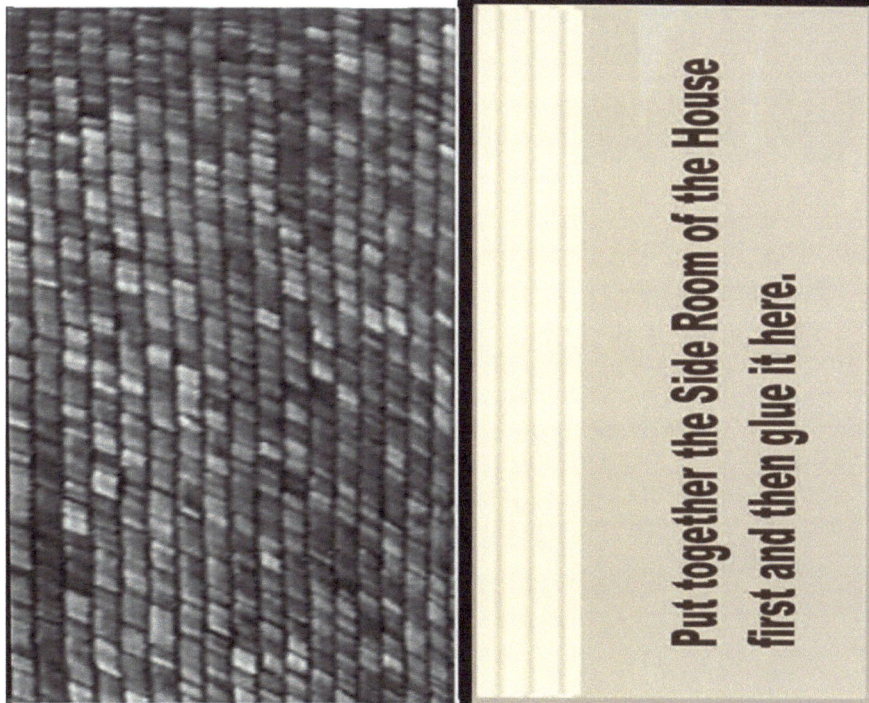

Put together the Side Room of the House first and then glue it here.

DOCK HOUSE   Page B

Family in the wagon.
Fold the photo
in half. Fold the
tan TABs outward.
Glue into the wagon.

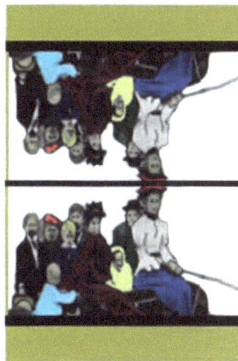

**Fold the wagon body into a box
and glue the ends together. Fold
the TABs under the wagon and place
the floor on the TABs with glue.**

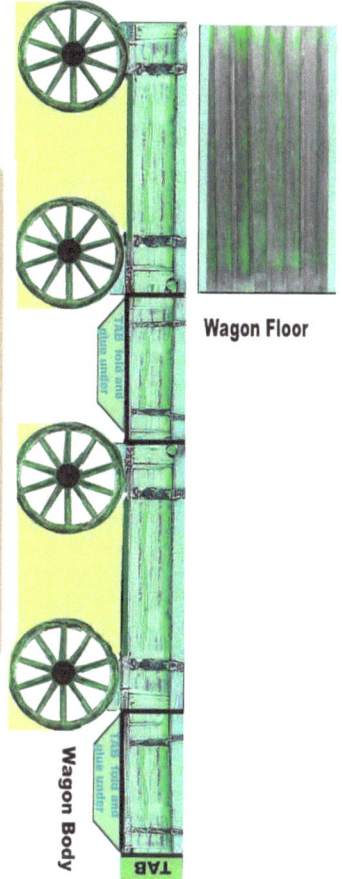

Wagon Floor

TAB

Wagon Body

TAB

**Glue the
wagon floor
to the TABs
as shown
here.**

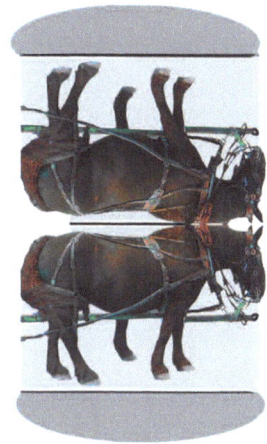

TAB

TAB

**Fold the two
horse images
together.
Fold the dark
gray ovals
outward to
form a
stand.**

Overlap
front porch.
Glue here.

Side Porch.
Fold outward
and glue on top
of Porch Roof TAB.

TAB
Glue to House Front

HOUSE BACK

DOCK HOUSE
Page C

SIDE ROOM PIECE

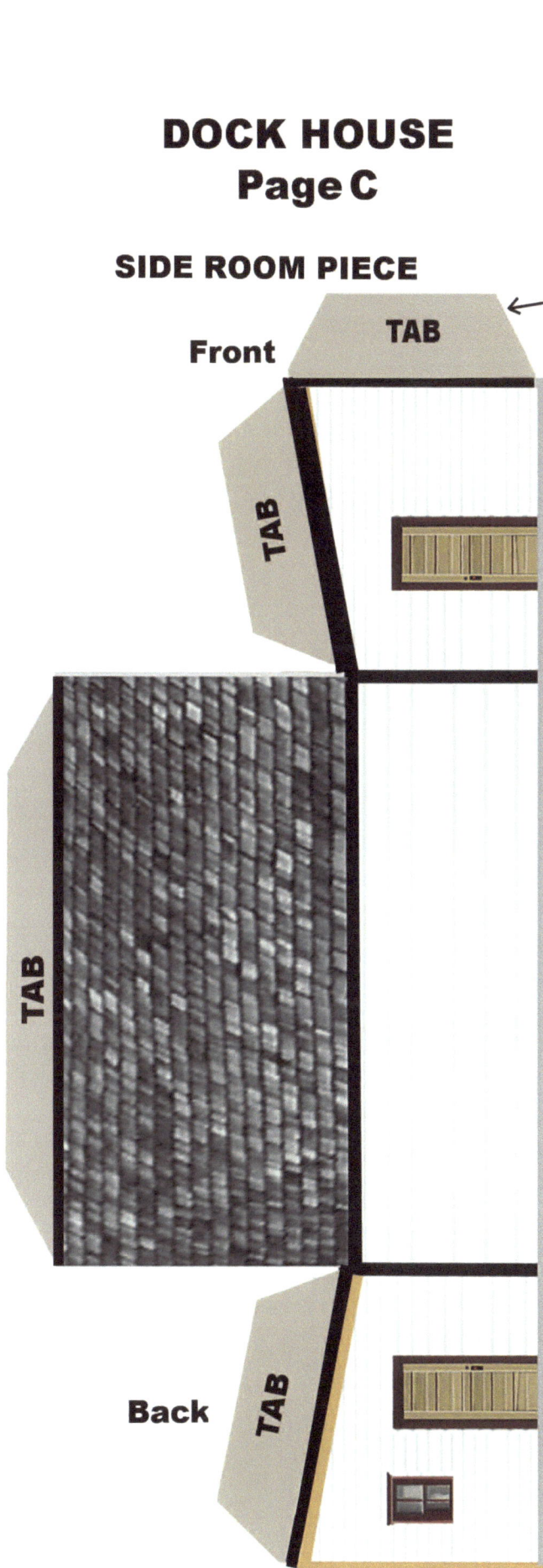

Front

TAB

TAB

TAB

TAB

Back

Glue this piece onto the Side Room Piece, then fold it to make a "box."

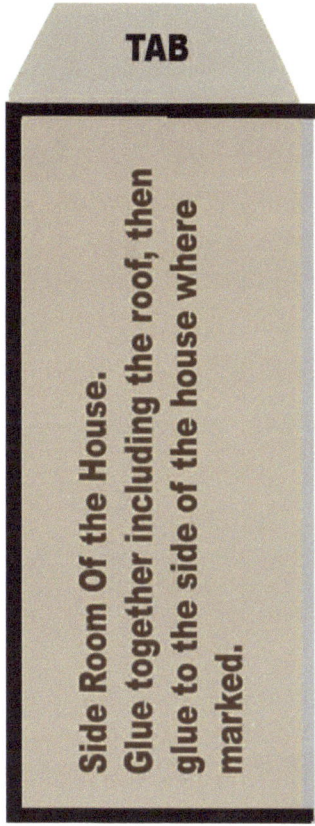

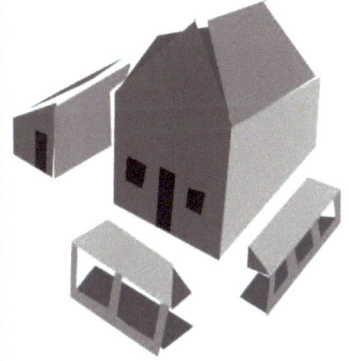

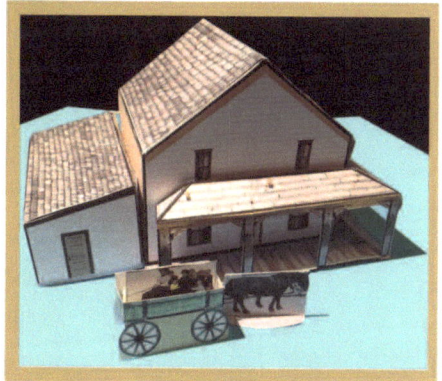

TAB

Side Room Of the House. Glue together including the roof, then glue to the side of the house where marked.

This is a photo of the finished model of the Dock House.

PORCH RAIL PIECE 2

(Add to the end of Porch Rail Piece 1.)

21

TAB

TAB Fold under. Glue to House.

TAB

Cut out this space.

Cut out this space.

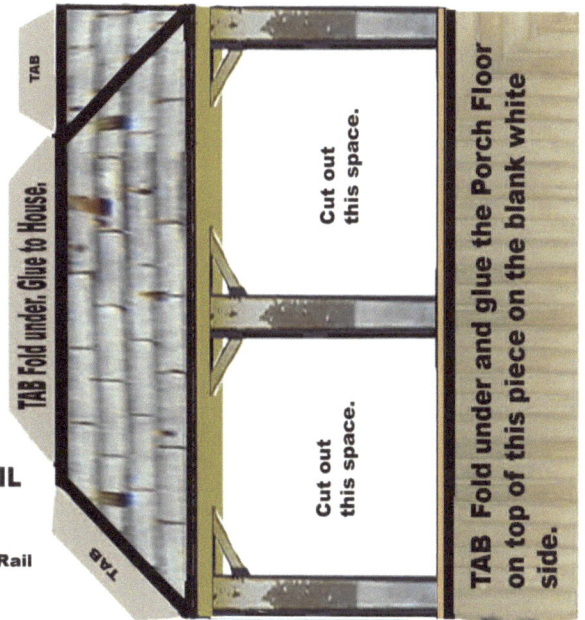

TAB Fold under and glue the Porch Floor on top of this piece on the blank white side.

HOBERT STORE
Page A

Doorway
Fold on black lines and glue to the entry TABs.

Glue door into place as shown in these two pictires

Front

Back

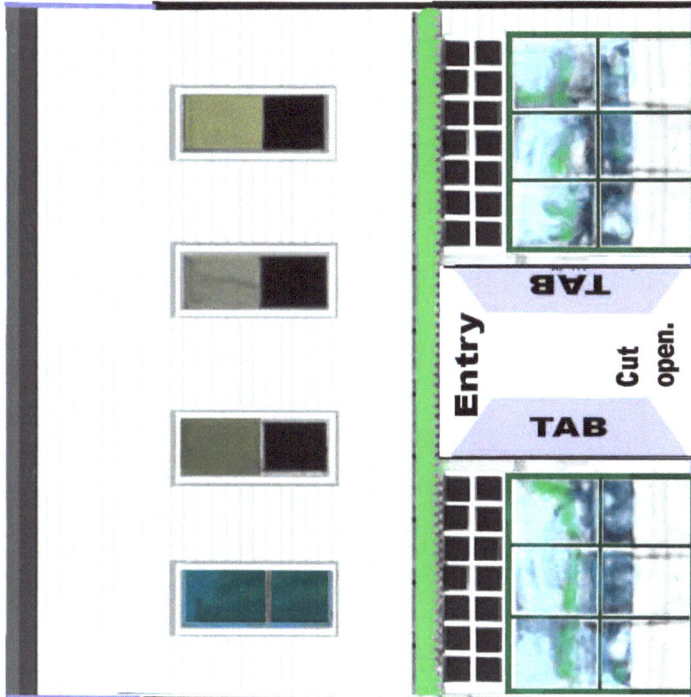

Entry

TAB

TAB

Cut open.

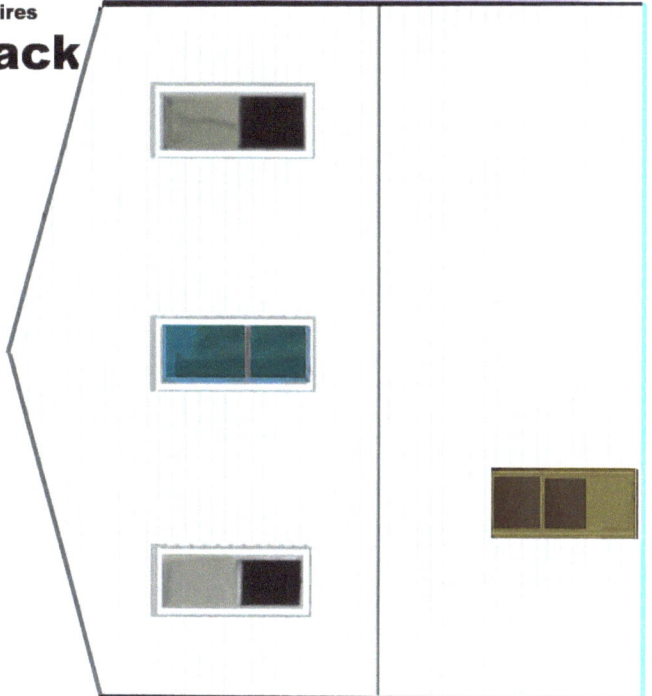

TAB

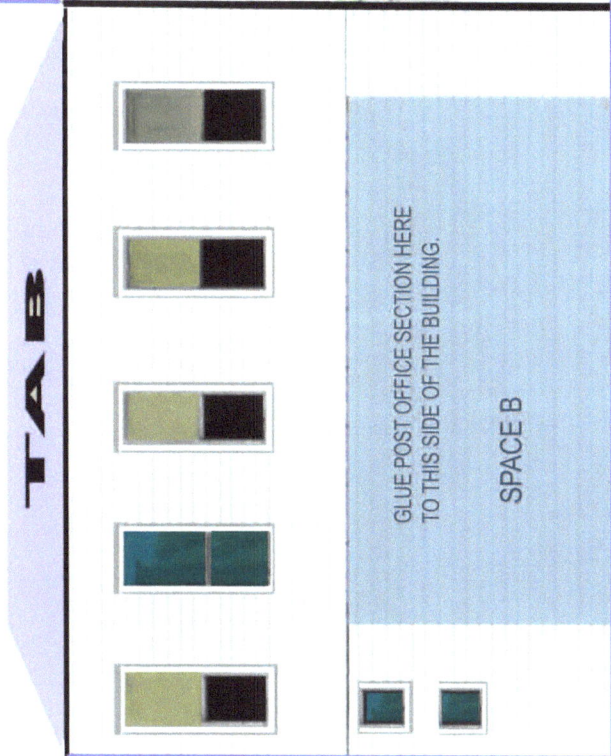

TAB

GLUE POST OFFICE SECTION HERE TO THIS SIDE OF THE BUILDING.

SPACE B

Glue the Front and Back pieces together. Fold them into a box.

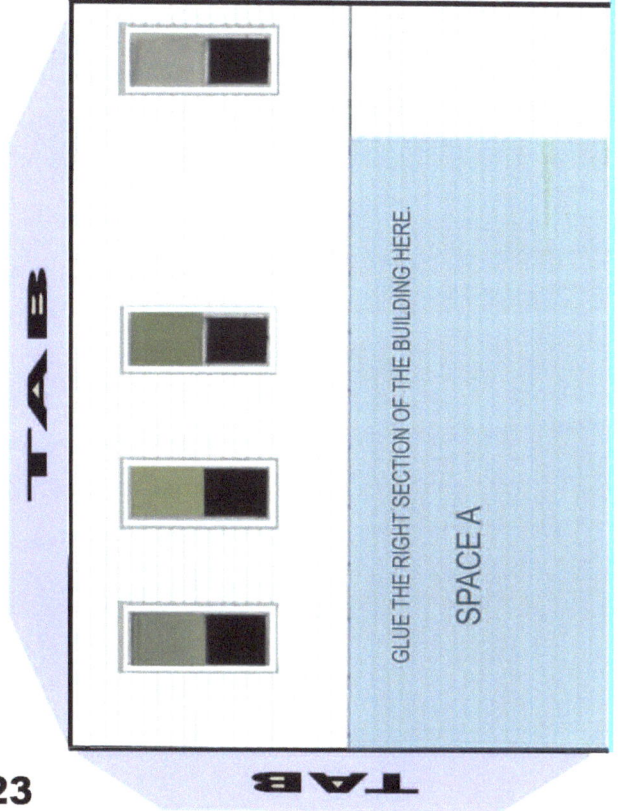

TAB

TAB

GLUE THE RIGHT SECTION OF THE BUILDING HERE.

SPACE A

23

Photos of the real Hobert Store

This is a photo of the original Hobert Store. It was also owned by the Kane Brothers at one time.

GLUE THE PEOPLE TO THE PORCH

TAB-FOLD UNDER

BOARDWALK

Put this TAB under the right part of the building

People in front of the store.

Put this TAB under the Main part of the store.

Glue Tab E here.

Put this TAB under the Post Office.

MAIN ROOF SECTION

This photo is the real people who were standing outside the Hobert Store in the photo on this page.

HOBERT STORE
Page C

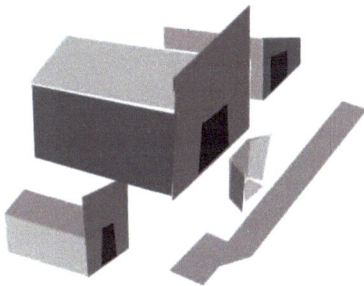

TAB Glue to roof.

This is a photo of the finished model of the Hobert Store.

Cut this little slit here.

TAB x

LACENTER POST OFFICE

TAB

STORAGE ROOM

Cut this little slit here.

POST OFFICE

TAB

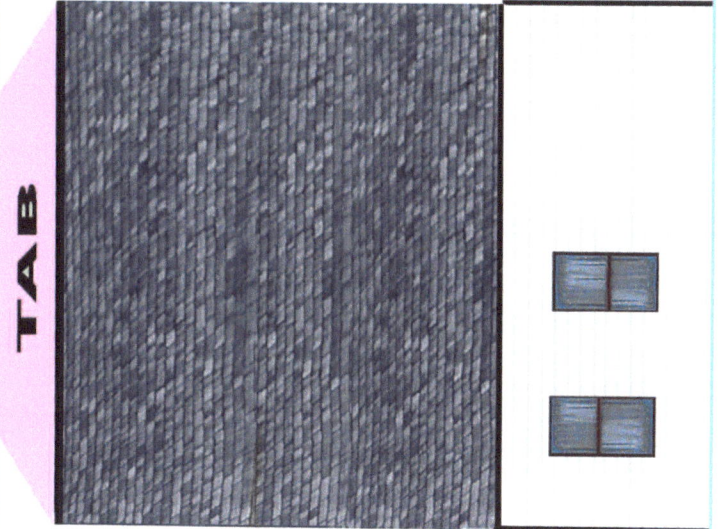

TAB Glue to roof.

Glue lavender section here.

RIGHT SECTION
Glue this wall to Space A.

Glue TAB here.

Glue blue section here.

Add this blue piece to this end of the Storage Room. Then fold the Storage Room into a "box" and glue it to the side of the store.

After you glue this Post Office section together, then glue it to the side of the main building here in the shaded area.

POST OFFICE SECTION

Glue TAB x here.

Add this blue piece to this end of the Post Office. Then fold the Post Office into a "box" and glue it to the side of the store.

27

Photo of
Steamboat
"La Center"
at the
La Center
Dock in 1912

Main Deck

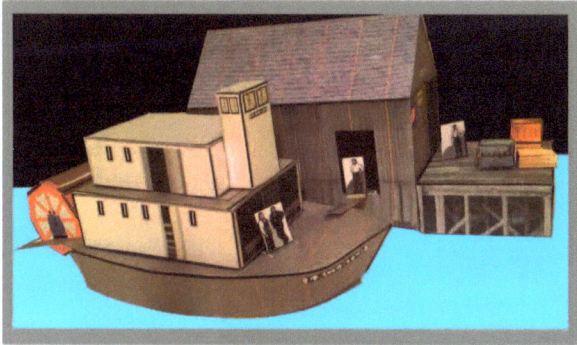

This is a photo of the finished
models of the Steamboat and
the Dock Building.

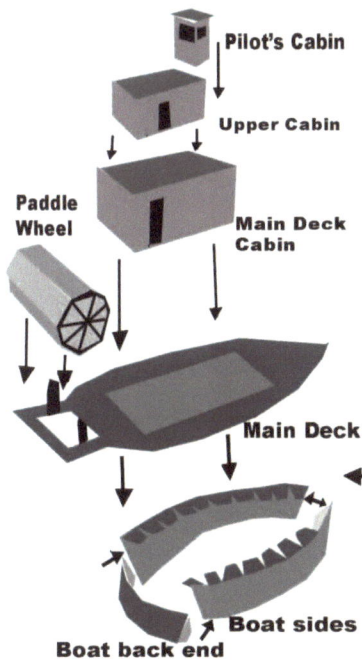

Pilot's Cabin

Upper Cabin

Paddle
Wheel

Main Deck
Cabin

Put the
Steamboat
together
like this.

Main Deck

Boat sides

Boat back end

29

Glue Main Deck Cabin here.

Cut
this
white
space
out.

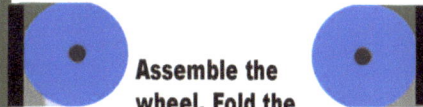

Assemble the
wheel. Fold the
blue circles upward.
Glue the wheel
between the two
blue circles.

Boat Side 1

Boat Side 2

Front

TAB

These are TABS. Glue the Main Deck to them.

Front

Clip when you need to. Use tape to hold while you glue the TABs.

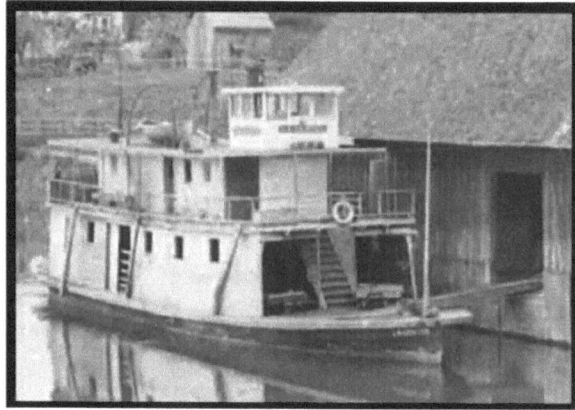

Photo of the real Steamboat "La Center" at the La Center Dock in 1917, after the boat had been remodelled.

Glue Boat Sides 1 and 2 together with the TAB at the front. Fold down the small TABs that run along the tops of the sides. Glue the Main Deck to these TABs, curving them to fit the edge of the deck. Glue the Back End to the Boat Sides across the back of the boat.

Back end of boat.

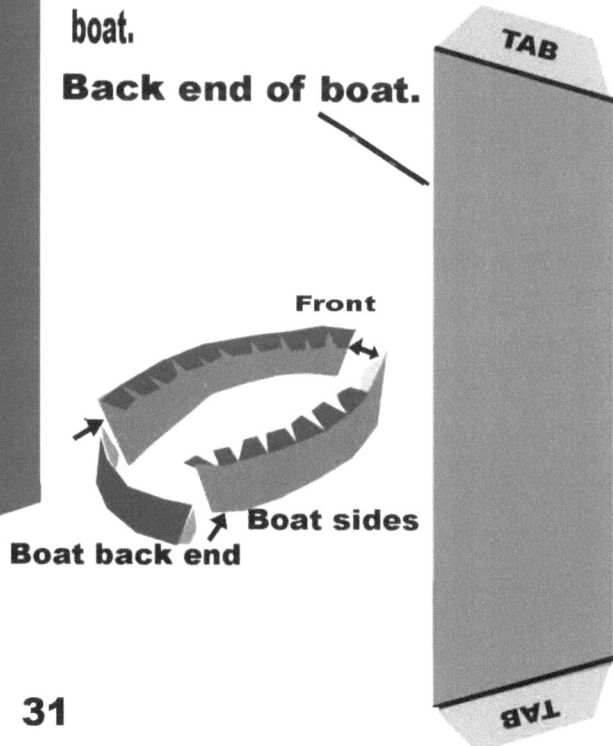

TAB

Front

Boat sides

Boat back end

TAB

Glue these two pieces end to end to make one long piece. Then fold the long piece into a "box."

Main Deck Cabin.

Fold into a box shape.
Fold the bottom TABs under and glue them to the floor of the main deck.

First, glue the two pieces together.

Then fold on black lines to make a "box."

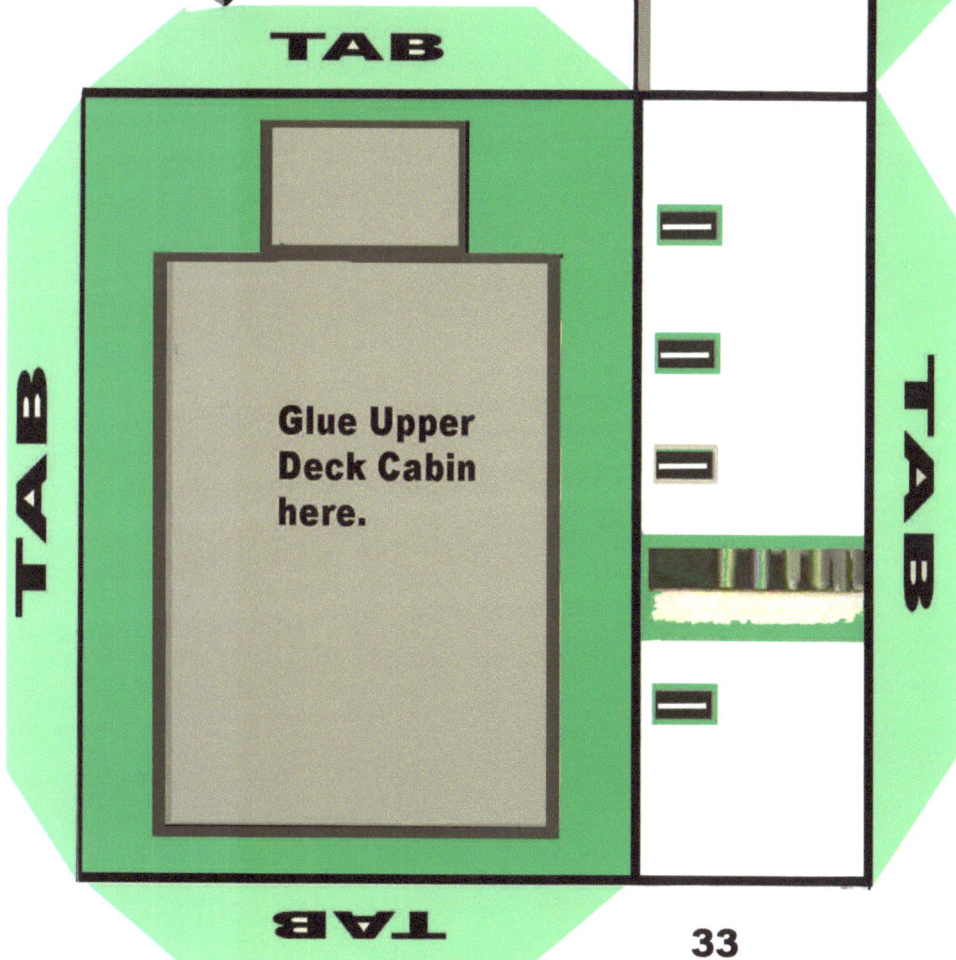

Back

Fold bottom TABS under to glue to the layer underneath.

TAB

Back

TAB

Front

TAB

TAB

TAB

TAB

TAB

TAB

TAB

Glue Upper Deck Cabin here.

TAB

Men Standing on the Main Deck.

STEAMBOAT "LA CENTER" Page D

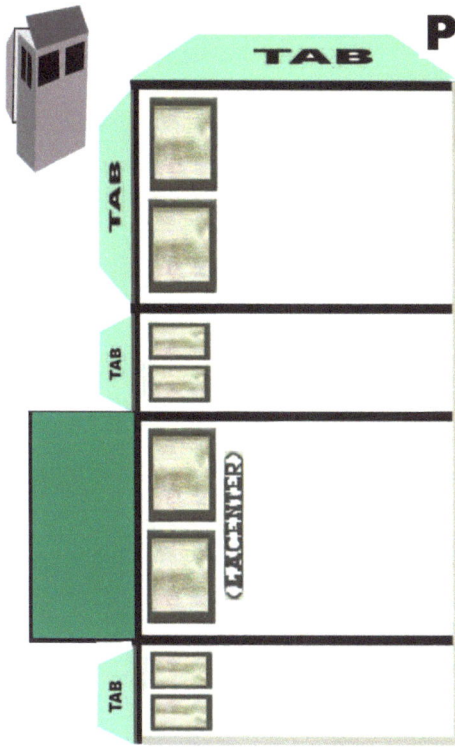

Pilot's Cabin

Fold into a box and glue to the front of the Upper Cabin.

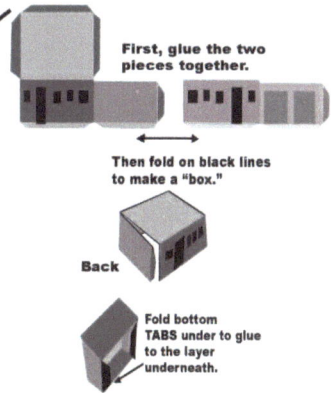

First, glue the two pieces together.

Then fold on black lines to make a "box."

Back

Fold bottom TABS under to glue to the layer underneath.

TAB

TAB

TAB

TAB

TAB

TAB

TAB

⟨LA CENTER⟩

Front

Glue Pilot's Cabin here.

TAB

TAB

Upper Cabin

Back

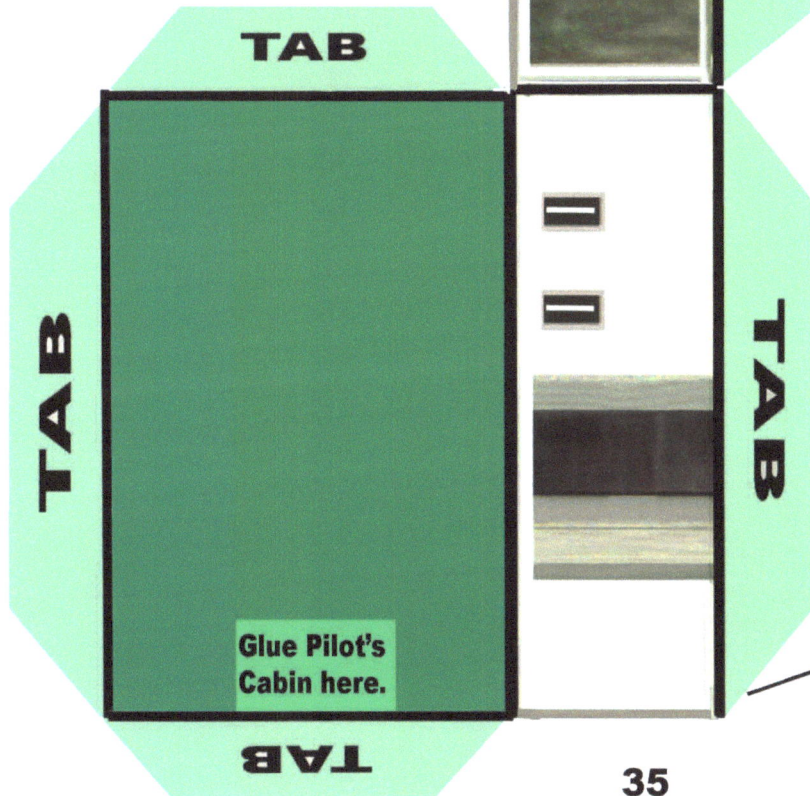

TAB

TAB

TAB

TAB

TAB

Glue Pilot's Cabin here.

Glue these two pieces end to end to make one long piece. Then fold the long piece into a "box."

Fold into a box shape. Fold the bottom TABs under and glue them to the floor of the upper deck.

35

STEAMBOAT "LA CENTER" Page E

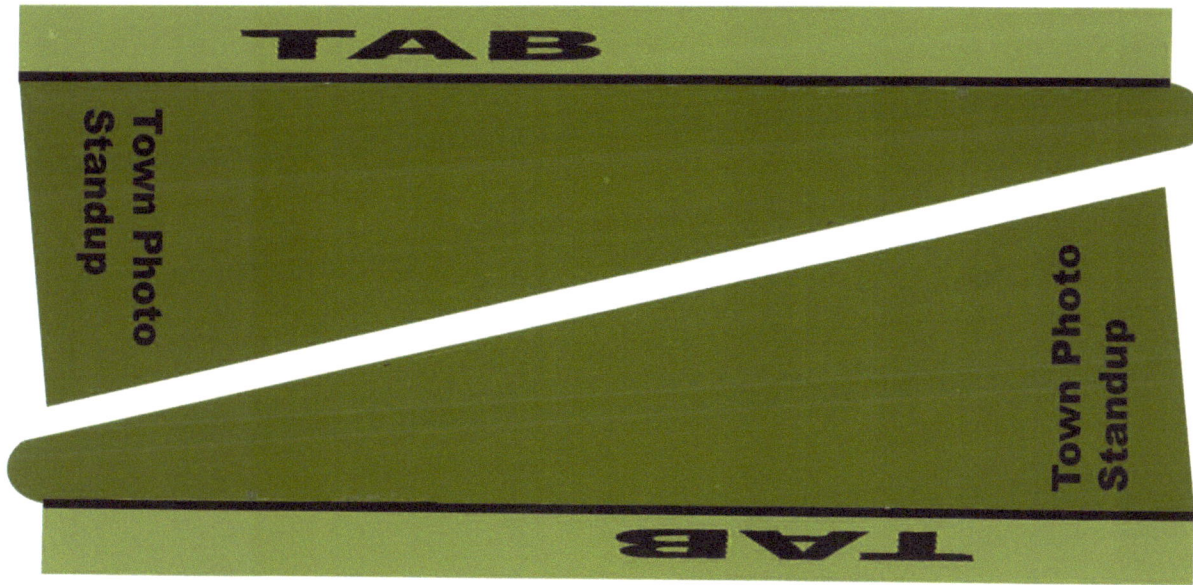

Town Photo Standup

TAB

Town Photo Standup

TAB

Back of Town Photo

Paddle Wheel

If you want: You may cut out the white inside each paddle and fold the red blade downward.

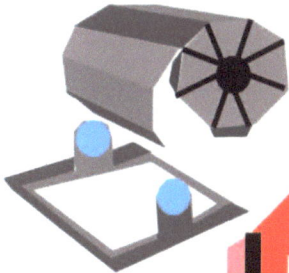

TAB

TAB

TAB

TAB

TAB

TAB

Fold on all black lines. Glue TABs to make a cylinder.

This is one paddle of eight on the wheel.

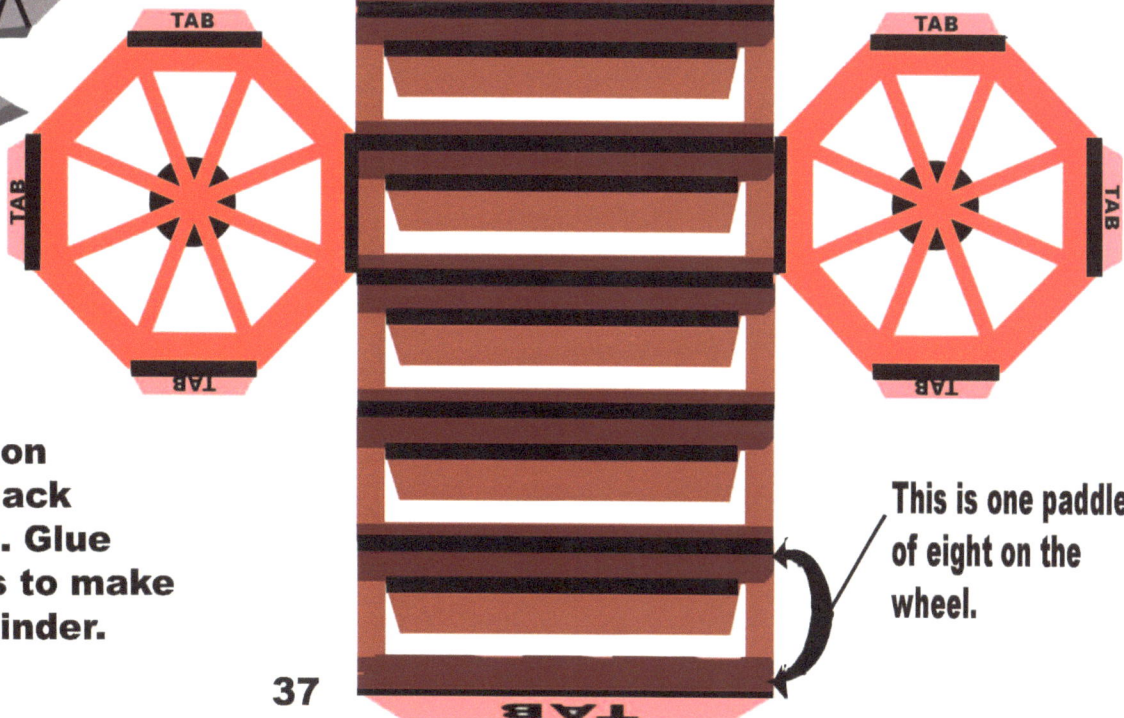

37

TAB

www.ingramcontent.com/pod-product-compliance
Lightning Source LLC
Chambersburg PA
CBHW042101040426
42448CB00002B/90